LOVER'S GIFT AND CROSSING

LOVER'S GIFT AND CROSSING

Rabindranath Tagore

Preface and introduction by
Bob DCosta

BLACK EAGLE BOOKS
Dublin, USA | Bhubaneswar, India

Black Eagle Books
  USA address:
7464 Wisdom Lane
Dublin, OH 43016

India address:
E/312, Trident Galaxy, Kalinga Nagar,
Bhubaneswar-751003, Odisha, India

E-mail: info@blackeaglebooks.org
Website: www.blackeaglebooks.org

First International Edition Published by
Black Eagle Books, 2023

LOVER'S GIFT AND CROSSING
by **Rabindranath Tagore**

Preface and introduction by **Bob DCosta**

Copyright © Author

All rights reserved. No part of this publication may be reproduced, stored in a retrieval system, or transmitted, in any form or by any means, electronic, mechanical, photocopying, recording or otherwise without the prior permission of the publisher.

Cover & Interior Design: Ezy's Publication

ISBN- 978-1-64560-425-9 (Paperback)

Printed in the United States of America

CONTENTS

Preface	09
Introduction / Bob DCosta	11

LOVER'S GIFT

You allowed your kingly power	15
Come to my garden walk	16
The fruits come in crowds	17
She is near to my heart	18
I would ask for still more	19
In the light of this thriftless	20
It is little that remains now	21
There is room for you	22
Woman, your basket is heavy	23
What is it that drives these bees	24
It was only the budding	25
Ages ago when you opened	26
Last night in the garden	27
If I am impatient to-day, forgive me	28
Her neighbours call her dark	29
She dwelt here by the pool	30
While ages passed and the bees	31
Your days will be full of cares	32
It is written in the book, that Man	33
Where is the market for you, my song?	34
Methinks, my love, before the daybreak	36
I shall gladly suffer the pride	37
I loved the sandy bank	39
Your window half opened	40
I clasp your hands, and my heart	41
If, by chance you think of me	42
I filled my tray with whatever	43
I dreamt that she sat by my head	44
I thought I had something to say	45
The spring flowers break out	46
My flowers were like milk	47
Many a time when the spring	48

The boisterous spring	49
When our farewell moment	50
Last night clouds were threatening	51
My fetters, you made music in my heart	52
You had your rudder broken	53
The current in which I drifted	54
There is a looker-on who sits	55
A message came from my youth	56
The girls are out to fetch water	57
Are you a mere picture	59
Dying, you have left behind	61
When in your death you died	62
Bring beauty and order into my	63
The sky gazes on its own endless blue	64
The road is my wedded companion	65
I travelled the old road every day	66
Where is heaven? you ask me	67
"Come, moon, come down,	68
The early autumn day is cloudless	69
Tired of waiting, you burst your bonds	70
I opened my bud when April breathed	71
In the beginning of time, there rose	72
The noonday air is quivering, like	73
The evening was lonely for me	74
This autumn is mine, for she was rocked	75
Things throng and laugh loud in the sky	76
They do not build high towers	77
Take back your coins, King's	79

CROSSING

The Sun breaks out from the clouds	85
When the market is over and they return	86
The wind is up, I set my sail of songs	87
Accept me, my lord, accept	88
The scouts of a distant storm	89
Thou hast done well, my lover	90
Deliver me from my own shadows	91

The lantern which I carry	92
When thou savest me the steps	93
Thou hast given me thy love	94
My eyes have lost their sleep	95
Hold thy faith firm, my heart	96
The wedding hour is in the twilight	97
In the night when noise is tired	98
Who is awake all alone in this sleeping	99
You came to my door in the dawn	100
Pick up this life of mine	101
I know that this life, missing	102
You came to me in the wayward	103
The day is dim with rain	104
On that night when the storm	105
Is it the Destroyer who comes?	106
I CAME nearest to you	107
Have you come	108
I HID myself to evade you	109
When I awake in thy love	110
I AM the weary earth of summer	111
Come to me like summer	112
I HAVE met thee where the night	113
If love be denied me then	114
Only a portion of my gift	115
I KNOW you will win my heart	116
Someone has secretly left	117
The rains sweep the sky	118
When I travelled in the day	119
Sailing through the night	120
Do not leave me and go	121
I DID not know that I had	122
No guest had come	123
Put out the lamps, my heart	124
Thy gift of the earliest flower	125
Free me as free are the birds	126
When you called me I was asleep	127
Rejoice !	128
In this moment I see you seated	129

My guest has come to my door	130
I LIVED on the shady side	131
Thou hast taken him to thine	132
In the world's dusty road	133
I WAS with the crowd	134
When they came and clamoured	135
Much have you given to me	136
I HAVE come to thee to take	137
Stand before my eyes	138
Let thy love play upon my voice	139
You hide yourself in your own	140
When from the house of feast	141
I WAS musing last night	142
None needs be thrust aside	143
With his morning songs	144
Run to his side as his comrades	145
When bells sounded in your temple	146
My King's road that lies still	147
While I walk to my King's	148
My songs are the same	149
My King, thou hast called	150
When my first early songs	151
There are numerous	152
Let my song be simple as the waking	153
I HAVE seen thee play thy music	154
I REMEMBER my childhood when	155
When my heart did not kiss	156
Thou hast given me thy seat	157
It has fallen upon me, the service	158
Guests of my life. You came in the early	159
I FELT I saw your face	160
"Traveller, where do you go?"	161
Comrade of the road	163
A short biography of Rabindranath Tagore	164

Preface

When Tagore was born, Bengal was waking up to a new life to find expression in three great movements – religious, literary, and national. These were later to be enriched by Tagore's own contributions. The religious movement was heralded by the 'great-hearted man of gigantic intelligence', as Tagore called him. Raja Ram Mohan Roy (1774 – 1833) the founder of the Brahma Samaj or 'Theistic Church of India'.

Roy made an endeavour to reopen the channel of spiritual life which had become obstructed and was screaming for spiritual significance. His was a strictly monotheistic religion based upon the religious teachings of the *Upanishads*. Believing in the harmony of religion, He taught reverence for all the great religions of the world. A true democrat, he worked hard for India's political and social advancement. Roy stood as the greatest influence in moulding Tagore's own ideal and in later addresses, Tagore expressed his deep indebtedness to him. Tagore's father Maharshi Devendranath became the leader of the Brahma Samaj after Ram Mohan Roy's demise, and for this reason the Tagore family was completely ostracized by orthodox

Hindus. However, Tagore remarked this as a blessing for him for it saved him from blindly imitating the past.

The second movement was heralded by the novelist Bankim Chandra Chatterjee (1838 to 1884) who breathed new life into the dying literature of Bengal. Tagore says of him as lifting the dead weight of labouriously heavy-footed forms from our Bengali language and with his magical touch stirring awake our literature from her age-long slumber.

Thirdly the national movement expressed a spirit of revolt and self-assertion against the political as well as the cultural dominance of the West. A generation of Indians who had grown up under a system of overseas education had blindly rejected their Indian cultural inheritance. Then the National Movement raised it head, aiming to rediscover India's soul and revived her arts and craft, introduced new industries and brought new life into the decaying villages.

All these three movements found active supporters in the Tagore family, among the poet's older brothers and cousins. In this challenging and invigorating environment, the boy Rabindranath grew up, absorbing the music, drama and poetry that often wafted in the air of the great Tagore mansion; and it was here, while still in his teens, began the poet's apprenticeship under the able guidance of his soul to carve on the stone of literature immortal creativity. From now on until almost the end of his life, a steady stream of poetry, drama, short stories, novels, literary criticism, social and political essays, religious and philosophical discourses poured out from Tagore's literary pen and gifting us unique education to continuously shine on the milky-way of Indian and world literature.

Introduction

To all of us lovers of literature, Tagore is the soul of poetry, and he is a true poet's soul. No wonder the bard of Bengal is popularly known as Kavi Guru all over the world, and we all find ourselves mere dots among the vastness of his literary work. And as for me, it has been nothing less than a celestial delight to read Lover's Gift and Crossing and write this preface and introduction.

Like all of us I had even been overwhelmed by Tagore's genius. Something stands out in recollection… While as a 5-year-old, I am busy in the world of reading my kindergarten book and moving my finger over "ABC Tumble down D/ the cat's in the cupboard and can't see me", the song from the transistor in the book shelf flowing out gently is "Gram chhara oi ranga matir poth/ Amar mon Bholai re" (That red-soiled path leading from the village/ Lures and makes me lose my mind). And as I am busy reading the alphabets, my subconscious mind, intoxicated with this song, hums it continuously.

This was my first tryst with Tagore's work, followed by *Jal parey pata norey* (Water drips/ leaves move). These were adequate for Kavi Guru to enter my little hut of a heart.

W. B. Yeats had rightly said, 'Whatever of philosophy has been made permanent is alone in poetry.' In his Hibbert lectures, Tagore had remarked: 'My religion is the religion of a poet. What I am going to say here comes out of an inner vision and not from knowledge.'

Lover's Gift and Crossing remains in the public domain, and I find it a great spiritual awakening of humility to present this masterpiece to poets and readers.

Kolkata, July, 2023 **Bob DCosta**

LOVER'S GIFT

1

You allowed your kingly power to vanish, Shajahan, but your wish was to make imperishable a tear-drop of love. Time has no pity for the human heart, he laughs at its sad struggle to remember.

You allured him with beauty, made him captive, and crowned the formless death with fadeless form.

The secret whispered in the hush of night to the ear of your love is wrought in the perpetual silence of stone.

Though empires crumble to dust, and centuries are lost in shadows, the marble still sighs to. the stars, "I remember."

"I remember."—But life forgets, for she has her call to the Endless: and she goes on her voyage unburdened, leaving her memories to the forlorn forms of beauty.

2

Come to my garden walk, my love. Pass by the fervid flowers that press themselves on your sight. Pass them by, stopping at some chance joy, that like a sudden wonder of sunset illumines, yet eludes.

For love's gift is shy, it never tells its name, it flits across the shade, spreading a shiver of joy along the dust. Overtake it or miss it for ever. But a gift that can be grasped is merely a frail flower, or a lamp with a flame that will flicker.

3

The fruits come in crowds into my orchard, they jostle each other. They surge up in the light in an anguish of fullness.

Proudly step into my orchard, my queen, sit there in the shade, pluck the ripe fruits from their stems, and let them yield, to the utmost, their burden of sweetness at your lips.

In my orchard the butterflies shake their wings in the sun, the leaves tremble, the fruits clamour to come to completion.

4

She is near to my heart as the meadow-flower to the earth; she is sweet to me as sleep is to tired limbs. My love for her is my life flowing in its fullness, like a river in autumn flood, running with serene abandonment. My songs are one with my love, like the murmur of a stream, that sings with all its waves and currents.

5

I would ask for still more, if I had the sky with all its stars, and the world with its endless riches; but I would be content with the smallest corner of this earth if only she were mine.

6

In the light of this thriftless day of spring, my poet, sing of those who pass by and do not linger, who laugh as they run and never look back, who blossom in an hour of unreasoning delight, and fade in a moment without regret.

Do not sit down silently, to tell the beads of your past tears and smiles,—do not stop to pick up the dropped petals from the flowers of overnight, do not go to seek things that evade you, to know the meaning that is not plain,—leave the gaps in your life where they are, for the music to come out of their depths.

7

It is little that remains now, the rest was spent in one careless summer. It is just enough to put in a song and sing to you; to weave in a flower-chain gently clasping your wrist; to hang in your ear like a round pink pearl, like a blushing whisper; to risk in a game one evening and utterly lose.

My boat is a frail small thing, not fit for crossing wild waves in the rain. If you but lightly step on it I shall gently row you by the shelter of the shore, where the dark water in ripples are like a dream-ruffled sleep; where the dove's cooing from the drooping branches makes the noon-day shadows plaintive. At the day's end, when you are tired, I shall pluck a dripping lily to put in your hair and take my leave.

8

There is room for you. You are alone with your few sheaves of rice. My boat is crowded, it is heavily laden, but how can I turn you away? Your young body is slim and swaying; there is a twinkling smile in the edge of your eyes, and your robe is coloured like the rain-cloud.

The travellers will land for different roads and homes. You will sit for a while on the prow of my boat, and at the journey's end none will keep you back.

Where do you go, and to what home, to garner your sheaves. I will not question you, but when I fold my sails and moor my boat, I shall sit and wonder in the evening, --Where do you go, and to what home, to garner your sheaves?

9

Woman, your basket is heavy, your limbs are tired. For what distance have you set out, with what hunger of profit? The way is long and the dust is hot in the sun.

See, the lake is deep and full, its water dark like a crow's eye. The banks are sloping and tender with grass.

Dip your tired feet into the water. The noontide wind will pass its fingers through your hair; the pigeons will croon their sleep songs, the leaves will murmur the secrets that nestle in the shadows.

What matters it if the hours pass and the sun sets; if the way through the desolate land be lost in the waning light.

Yonder is my house, by the hedge of flowering henna; I will guide you. I will make a bed for you, and light a lamp. In the morning when the birds are roused by the stir of milking the cows, I will waken you.

10

What is it that drives these bees from their home; these followers of unseen trails? What cry is this in their eager wings? How can they hear the music that sleeps in the flower soul? How can they find their way to the chamber where the honey lies shy and silent?

11

It was only the budding of leaves in the summer, the summer that came into the garden by the sea. It was only a stir and rustle in the south wind, a few lazy snatches of songs, and then the day was done.

But let there be flowering of love in the summer to come in the garden by the sea. Let my joy take its birth and clap its hands and dance with the surging songs, and make the morning open its eyes wide in sweet amazement.

12

Ages ago when you opened the south gate of the garden of gods, and came down upon the first youth of the earth, O Spring; men and women rushed out of their houses, laughing and dancing, and pelting each other with flower-dust in a sudden madness of mirth.

Year after year you bring the same flowers that you scattered in your path in that earliest April. Therefore, to-day, in their pervading perfume, they breathe the sigh of the days that are now dreams, — the clinging sadness of vanished worlds. Your breeze is laden with love-legends that have faded from all human language.

One day, with fresh wonder, you came into my life that was fluttered with its first love. Since then the tender timidness of that inexperienced joy comes hidden every year in the early green buds of your lemon flowers; your red roses carry in their burning silence all that was unutterable in me; the memory of lyric hours, those days of May, rustles in the thrill of your new leaves born again and again.

13

Last night in the garden I offered you my youth's foaming wine. You lifted the cup to your lips, you shut your eyes and smiled while I raised your veil, unbound your tresses, drawing down upon my breast your face sweet with its silence, last night when the moon's dream overflowed the world of slumber.

To-day in the dew-cooled calm of the dawn you are walking to God's temple, bathed and robed white, with a basketful of flowers in your hand. I stand aside in the shade under the tree, with my head bent, in the calm of the dawn by the lonely road to the temple.

14

If I am impatient to-day, forgive me, my love. It is the first summer rain, and the riverside forest is aflutter, and the blossoming kadam trees, are tempting the passing winds with wine-cups of perfume. See, from all corners of the sky lightnings are darting their glances, and winds are rampant in your hair.

If to-day I bring my homage to you, forgive me, my love. The everyday world is hidden in the dimness of the rain, all work has stopped in the village, the meadows are desolate. In your dark eyes the coming of the rain finds its music, and it is at your door that July waits with jasmines for your hair in its blue skirt.

15

Her neighbours call her dark in the village — but she is a lily to my heart, yes, a lily though not fair. Light came muffled with clouds, when first I saw her in the field; her head was bare, her veil was off, her braided hair hanging loose on her neck. She may be dark as they say in the village, but I have seen her black eyes and am glad.

The pulse of the air boded storm. She rushed out of the hut, when she heard her dappled cow low in dismay. For a moment she turned her large eyes to the clouds, and felt a stir of the coming rain in the sky. I stood at the corner of the ricefield, — if she noticed me, it was known only to her (and perhaps I know it). She is dark as the message of shower in summer, dark as the shade of flowering woodland; she is dark as the longing for unknown love in the wistful night of May.

16

She dwelt here by the pool with its landing-stairs in ruins. Many an evening she had watched the moon made dizzy by the shaking of bamboo leaves, and on many a rainy day the smell of the wet earth had come to her over the young shoots of rice.

Her pet name is known here among those datepalm groves, and in the court-years where girls sit and talk, while stitching their winter quilts. The water in this pool keeps in its depth the memory of her swimming limbs, and her wet feet had left their marks, day after day, on the footpath leading to the village.

The women who come to-day with their vessels to the water, have all seen her smile over simple jests, and the old peasant, taking his bullocks to their bath, used to stop at her door every day to greet her.

Many a sailing boat passes by this village; many a traveller takes rest beneath that banyan tree; the ferry boat crosses to yonder ford carry- LOVER'S GIFT 23 ing crowds to the market; but they never notice this spot by the village road, near the pool with its ruined landing-stairs,—where dwelt she whom I love.

17

While ages passed and the bees haunted the summer gardens, the moon smiled to the skies of the night, the lightnings flashed their fiery kisses to the clouds and fled laughing, the poet stood in a corner, one with the trees and clouds. He kept his heart silent, like a flower, watched through his dreams as does the crescent moon; and wandered like the summer breeze for no purpose.

One April evening, when the moon rose up like a bubble from the depth of the sunset; and one maiden was busy watering the plants; and one feeding her doe, and one making her peacock dance, the poet broke out singing, "O listen to the secrets of the world. I know that the lily is pale for the moon's love. The lotus draws her veil aside before the morning sun, and the reason is simple if you think. The meaning of the bee's hum in the ear of the early jasmine has escaped the learned, but the poet knows."

The sun went down in a blaze of blush, the moon loitered behind the trees, and the south wind whispered to the lotus, that the poet was not as simple as he seemed. The maidens and youths clapped their hands and cried, "The world's secret is out." They looked into each other's e^^es and sang—"Let our secret as well be flung into the winds."

18

Your days will be full of cares, if you must give me your heart. My house by the cross-roads has its doors open and my mind is absent, for I sing.

I shall never be made to answer for it, if you must give me your heart. If I pledge my word to you in tunes now, and am too much in earnest to keep it when music is silent, you must forgive me; for the law laid in May is best broken in December.

Do not always keep remembering it, if you must give me your heart. When your eyes sing with love, and your voice ripples with laughter, my answers to your questions will be wild, and not miserly accurate in facts, they are to be believed for ever and then forgotten for good.

19

It is written in the book, that Man, when fifty, must leave the noisy world, to go to the forest seclusion. But the poet proclaims that only for the young is the forest hermitage. For it is the birth-place of flowers, and the haunt of birds and bees; and hidden nooks are waiting there for the thrill of lover's whispers. There the moonlight, that is all one kiss for the malati flowers, has its deep message, but those who understand it are far below fifty.

And alas, youth is inexperienced and wilful, therefore it is but meet, that the old should take charge of the household, and the young take to the seclusion of forest shades, and the severe discipline of courting.

20

Where is the market for you, my song? Is it there where the learned muddle the summer breeze with their snuff; where dispute is unending if the oil depend upon the cask, or the cask upon the oil; where yellow manuscripts frown upon the fleet-footed frivolousness of life? My song cries out. Ah, no, no, no.

Where is the market for you, my song? Is it there where the man of fortune grows enormous in pride and flesh in his marble palace, with his books on the shelves, dressed in leather, painted in gold, dusted by slaves, their virgin pages dedicated to the god obscure? My song gasped and said. Ah, no, no, no.

Where is the market for you, my song? Is it there where the young student sits, with his head bent upon his books, and his mind straying in youth's dream-land; where prose is prowling on the desk, and poetry hiding in the heart? There among that dusty disorder, would you care to play hide-and-seek? My song remains silent in shy hesitation.

Where is the market for you, my song? Is it there where the bride is busy in the house, where she runs to her bedroom the moment she is free, and snatches, from under her pillows, the book of romance so roughly handled by the baby, so full of the scent of her hair? My song heaves a sigh and trembles with uncertain desire. Where is the market for you, my song? Is it there where the least of a bird's notes is never missed, where the stream's babbling finds its full wisdom where all the lute-strings of the world shower their music upon two fluttering hearts? My song bursts out and cries, Yes, yes.

21

(From the Bengali of Devendranath Sen)
Methinks, my love, before the daybreak of life you stood under some waterfall of happy dreams, filling your blood with its liquid turbulence. Or, perhaps, your path was through the garden of the gods, where the merry multitude of jasmine, lilies, and oleanders fell in your arms in heaps, and entering your heart became boisterous.

Your laughter is a song whose words are drowned in the clamour of tune, a rapture of odour of flowers that are not seen; it is like the moonlight breaking through your lips' window when the moon is hiding in your heart. I ask for no reason, I forget the cause, I only know that your laughter is the tumult of insurgent life.

22

I shall gladly suffer the pride of culture to die out in my house, if only in some fortunate future I am born a herd boy in the Brinda forest.
he herd boy who grazes his cattle sitting under the banyan tree, and idly weaves gunja flowers into garlands, who loves to splash and plunge in the Jamuna's cool deep stream.

He calls his companions to wake up when morning dawns, and all the houses in the lane hum with the sound of the churn, clouds of dust are raised by the cattle, the maidens come out in the courtyard to milk the kine.

As the shadows deepen under the tomal trees, and the dusk gathers on the river-banks; when the milkmaids, while crossing the turbulent water, tremble with fear; and loud peacocks, with tails outspread, dance in the forest, he watches the summer clouds.

When the April night is sweet as a fresh-blown flower, he disappears in the forest with a peacock's plume in his hair; the swing ropes are twined with flowers on the branches; the south wind throbs with music, and the merry shepherd boys crowd on the banks of the blue river.
No, I will never be the leader, brothers, of this new age of

new Bengal; I shall not trouble to light the lamp of culture for the benighted. If only I could be born, under the shady Asoka groves, in some village of Brinda, where milk is churned by the maidens.

23

I loved the sandy bank where, in the lonely pools, ducks clamoured and turtles basked in the sun; where, with evening, stray fishing-boats took shelter in the shadow by the tall grass.

You loved the wooded bank where shadows were gathered in the arms of the bamboo thickets; where women came with their vessels through the winding lane.

The same river flowed between us, singing the same song to both its banks. I listened to it, lying alone on the sand under the stars; and you listened sitting by the edge of the slope in the early morning light. Only the words I heard from it you did not know and the secret it spoke to you was a mystery for ever to me.

24

Your window half opened and veil half raised you stand there waiting for the bangle-seller to come with his tinsel. You idly watch the heavy cart creak on in the dusty road, and the boatmast crawling along the horizon across the far-off river.

The world to you is like an old woman's chant at her spinning-wheel, unmeaning rhymes crowded with random images.

But who knows if he is on his way this lazy sultry noon, the Stranger, carrying his basket of strange wares. He will pass by your door with his clear cry, and you shall fling open your window, cast off your veil, come out of the dusk of your dreams and meet your destiny.

25

I clasp your hands, and my heart plunges into the dark of your eyes, seeking you, who ever evade me behind words and silence.

Yet I know that I must be content in my love, with what is fitful and fugitive. For we have met for a moment in the crossing of the roads. Have I the power to carry you through this crowd of worlds, through this maze of paths? Have I the food that can sustain you, across the dark passage gaping with arches of death?

26

If, by chance you think of me, I shall sing to you when the rainy evening loosens her shadows upon the river, slowly trailing her dim light towards the west, -- when the day's remnant is too narrow for work or for play.

You will sit alone in the balcony of the south, and I shall sing from the darkened room. In the growing dusk, the smell of the wet leaves will come through the window; and the stormy winds will become clamorous in the cocoanut grove.

When the lighted lamp is brought into the room I shall go. And then, perhaps, you will listen to the night, and hear my song when I am silent.

27

I filled my tray with whatever I had, and gave it to you. What shall I bring to your feet tomorrow, I wonder. I am like the tree that, at the end of the flowering summer, gazes at the sky with its lifted branches bare of their blossoms.

But in all my past offerings is there not a single flower made fadeless by the eternity of tears?

Will you remember it and thank me with your eyes when I stand before you with empty hands at the leave-taking of my summer days?

28

I dreamt that she sat by my head, tenderly ruffling my hair with her fingers, playing the melody of her touch. I looked at her face and struggled with my tears, till the agony of unspoken words burst my sleep like a bubble.

I sat up and saw the glow of the milky way above my window, like a world of silence on fire, and I wondered if at this moment she had a dream that rhymed with mine.

29

I thought I had something to say to her when our eyes met across the hedge. But she passed away. And it rocks day and night, like a boat, on every wave of the hours the word that I had to say to her. It seems to sail in the autumn clouds in an endless quest and to bloom into evening flowers seeking its lost moment in the sunset. It twinkles like fireflies in my heart to find its meaning in the dusk of despair the word that I had to say to her.

30

The spring flowers break out like the passionate pain of unspoken love. With their breath comes the memory of my old day songs. My heart of a sudden has put on green leaves of desire. My love came not but her touch is in my limbs, and her voice comes across the fragrant fields. Her gaze is in the sad depth of the sky, but where are her eyes? Her kisses flit in the air, but where are her lips?

31

A POSY (From the Bengali of Satyendranath Datta)

My flowers were like milk and honey and wine;
I bound them into a posy with a golden ribbon,
but they escaped my watchful care and fled away
and only the ribbon remains.

My songs were like milk and honey and wine,
they were held in the rhythm of my beating heart,
but they spread their wings and fled away,
the darlings of the idle hours,
and my heart beats in silence.

The beauty I loved was like milk and honey
and wine, her lips like the rose of the dawn, her
eyes bee-black. I kept my heart silent lest it
should startle her, but she eluded me like my
flowers and like my songs, and my love remains
alone.

32

Many a time when the spring day knocked at
our door I kept busy with my work and you did
not answer. Now when I am left alone and heart
-sick the spring day comes once again, but I know
not how to turn him away from the door.
When he came to crown us with joy the gate was shut,
but now when he comes with his gift of sorrow
his path must be open.

33

The boisterous spring, who once came into my life with its lavish laughter, burdening her hours with improvident roses, setting skies aflame with the red kisses of new-born ashoka leaves, now comes stealing into my solitude through the lonely lanes along the brooding shadows heavy with silence, and sits still in my balcony gazing across the fields, where the green of the earth swoons exhausted in the utter paleness of the sky.

34

When our farewell moment came, like a low-hanging rain cloud, I had only time to tie a red ribbon on your wrist, while my hands trembled. To-day I sit alone on the grass in the season of mahua flowers, with one quivering question in my mind, "Do you still keep the little red ribbon tied on your wrist?"

You went by the narrow road that skirted the blossoming field of flax. I saw that my garland of overnight was still hanging loose from your hair. But why did you not wait till I could gather, in the morning, new flowers for my final gift? I wonder if unaware it dropped on your way, — the garland hanging loose from your hair.

Many a song I had sung to you, morning and evening, and the last one you carried in your voice
when you went away. You never tarried to hear the one song unsung I had for you alone and for ever. I wonder if, at last, you are tired of my song that you hummed to yourself while walking through the field.

35

Last night clouds were threatening and *amlak* branches struggled in the grips of the gusty wind. I hoped, if dreams came to me, they would come in the shape of my beloved, in the lonely night loud with rain.

The winds still moan through the fields, and the tear-stained cheeks of dawn are pale. My dreams have been in vain, for truth is hard, and dreams, too, have their own ways.

Last night when the darkness was drunken with storm, and the rain, like night's veil, was torn by the winds into shreds, would it make truth jealous, if untruth came to me in the shape of my beloved, in the starless night loud with rain?

36

My fetters, you made music in my heart. I played with you all day long and made you my ornament. We were the best of friends, my fetters. There were times when I was afraid of you, but my fear made me love you the more. You were companions of my long dark night, and I make my bow to you, before I bid you good-bye, my fetters.

37

You had your rudder broken many a time, my
boat, and your sails torn to tatters. Often had
you drifted towards the sea, dragging anchor and
heeded not. But now there has spread a crack
in your hull and your hold is heavy. Now is the
time for you to end your voyage, to be rocked
into sleep by the lapping of the water by the beach.

Alas, I know all warning is vain. The veiled
face of dark doom lures you. The madness of
the storm and the waves is upon you. The music
of the tide is rising high. You are shaken by the
fever of that dance.

Then break your chain, my boat, and be free,
and fearlessly rush to your wreck.

38

The current in which I drifted ran rapid and strong when I was young. The spring breeze was spendthrift of itself, the trees were on fire with flowers; and the birds never slept from singing.

I sailed with giddy speed, carried away by the flood of passion; I had no time to see and feel and take the world into my being.

Now that youth has ebbed and I am stranded on the bank, I can hear the deep music of all things, and the sky opens to me its heart of stars.

39

There is a looker-on who sits behind my eyes.
It seems he has seen things in ages and worlds
beyond memory's shore, and those forgotten
sights glisten on the grass, and shiver on the
leaves. He has seen under new veils the face
of the one beloved, in twilight hours of many a
nameless star. Therefore his sky seems to ache
with the pain of countless meetings and partings,
and a longing pervades this spring breeze,—
the longing that is full of the whisper of ages without
beginning.

40

A message came from my youth of vanished days, saying, "I wait for you among the quiverings of unborn May, where smiles ripen for tears and hours ache with songs unsung."

It says, "Come to me across the worn-out track of age, through the gates of death. For dreams fade, hopes fail, the gathered fruits of the year decay, but I am the eternal truth, and you shall meet me again and again in your voyage of life from shore to shore."

41

The girls are out to fetch water from the river —
their laughter comes through the trees, I long to
join them in the lane, where goats graze in the
shade, and squirrels flit from sun to shadow,
across the fallen leaves.

But my day's task is already done, my jars
are filled. I stand at my door to watch the glistening
green of the areca leaves, and hear the
laughing women going to fetch water from the
river.

It has ever been dear to me to carry the burden
of my full vessel day after day, in the dew-dipped
morning freshness and in the tired glimmer of
the dayfall.

Its gurgling water babbled to me when my
mind was idle, it laughed with the silent laughter
of my joyous thoughts—it spoke to my heart with
tearful sobs when I was sad. I have carried it
in stormy days, when the loud rain drowned the
anxious cooing of doves.

My day's task is done, my jars are filled, the light wanes in the west, and shadows gather beneath the trees; a sigh comes from the flowering linseed field, and my wistful eyes follow the lane, that runs through the village to the bank of the dark water.

42

Are you a mere picture, and not as true as those stars, true as this dust? They throb with the pulse of things, but you are immensely aloof in your stillness, painted form.

The day was when you walked with me, your breath warm, your limbs singing of life. My world found its speech in your voice, and touched my heart with your face. You suddenly stopped in your walk, in the shadow-side of the Forever, and I went on alone.

Life, like a child, laughs, shaking its rattle of death as it runs; it beckons me on, I follow the unseen; but you stand there, where you stopped behind that dust and those stars; and you are a mere picture.

No, it cannot be. Had the lifeflood utterly stopped in you, it would stop the river in its flow, and the footfall of dawn in her cadence of colours. Had the glimmering dusk of your hair vanished in the hopeless dark, the woodland shade of summer would die with its dreams.

Can it be true that I forgot you? We haste
on without heed, forgetting the flowers on the
roadside hedge. Yet they breathe unaware into
our forgetfulness, filling it with music.
You have moved from my world, to take seat at the
root of my life, and therefore is this forgetting —
remembrance lost in its own depth.

You are no longer before my songs, but one
with them. You came to me with the first ray
of dawn. I lost you with the last gold of evening.
Ever since I am always finding you through the
dark. No, you are no mere picture.

43

Dying, you have left behind you the great sadness
of the Eternal in my life. You have painted
my thought's horizon with the sunset colours of your
departure, leaving a track of tears across
the earth to love's heaven. Clasped in your
dear arms, life and death united in me in a marriage
bond.

I think I can see you watching there in the
balcony with your lamp lighted, where the end
and the beginning of all things meet. My world
went hence through the doors that you opened
— you holding the cup of death to my lips, filling
it with life from your own.

44

When in your death you died to all that was outside me, vanishing from the thousand things of the world, to be fully reborn in my sorrow, I felt that my life had grown perfect, the man and the woman becoming one in me for ever.

45

Bring beauty and order into my forlorn life,
woman, as you brought them into my house
when you lived. Sweep away the dusty fragments
of the hours, fill the empty jars and mend
all neglects. Then open the inner door of the
shrine, light the candle, and let us meet there in
silence before our God.

46

The sky gazes on its own endless blue and dreams.
We clouds are its whims, we have no home.
The stars shine on the crown of Eternity. Their
records are permanent, while ours are penciled,
to be rubbed off the next moment. Our part is
to appear on the stage of the air to sound our
tambourines and fling flashes of laughter.
But from our laughter comes the rain, which is real
enough, and thunder which is no jest. Yet we
have no claim upon Time for wages, and the
breath that blew us into being blows us away
before we are given a name.

47

The road is my wedded companion. She speaks to me under my feet all day, she sings to my dreams all night.

My meeting with her had no beginning, it begins endlessly at each daybreak, renewing its summer in fresh flowers and songs, and her every new kiss is the first kiss to me.

The road and I are lovers. I change my dress for her night after night, leaving the tattered cumber of the old in the wayside inns when the day dawns.

48

I travelled the old road every day, I took my
fruits to the market, my cattle to the meadows,
I ferried my boat across the stream and all the
ways were well known to me.

One morning my basket was heavy with wares.
Men were busy in the fields, the pastures crowded
with cattle; the breast of earth heaved with the
mirth of ripening rice.

Suddenly there was a tremor in the air,
and the sky seemed to kiss me on my
forehead. My mind started up like the morning out of mist.

I forgot to follow the track. I stepped a few
paces from the path, and my familiar world appeared
strange to me, like a flower I had only
known in bud.

My everyday wisdom was ashamed. I went
astray in the fairyland of things. It was the best
luck of my life, that I lost my path that morning,
and found my eternal childhood.

49

Where is heaven? you ask me, my child,—
the sages tell us it is beyond the limits of birth and
death, unswayed by the rhythm of day and
night; it is not of this earth.

But your poet knows that its eternal hunger
is for time and space, and it strives evermore to
be born in the fruitful dust. Heaven is fulfilled
in your sweet body, my child, in your palpitating
heart.

The sea is beating its drums in joy, the flowers
are a-tiptoe to kiss you. For heaven is born in
you, in the arms of the mother-dust.

50

THE CHILD (Translated from the Bengalin of Dwyendralal Roy)
"Come, moon, come down, kiss my darling on the forehead," cries the mother as she holds the baby girl in her lap while the moon smiles as it dreams. There come stealing in the dark the vague fragrance of the summer and the nightbird's songs from the shadow-laden solitude of the mango-grove. At a far-away village rises from a peasant's flute a fountain of plaintive notes, and the young mother, sitting on the terrace, baby in her lap, croons sweetly,
"Come, moon, come down, kiss my darling on the forehead."
Once she looks up at the light of the sky, and then at the light of the earth in her arms, and I wonder at the placid silence of the moon.

The baby laughs and repeats her mother's call, "Come, moon, come down." The mother smiles, and smiles the moonlit night, and I, the poet, the husband of the baby's mother, watch this picture from behind, unseen.

51

The early autumn day is cloudless. The river
is full to the brim, washing the naked roots of
the tottering tree by the ford. The long narrow
path, like the thirsty tongue of the village, dips
down into the stream.

My heart is full, as I look around me and
see the silent sky and the flowing water, and feel
that happiness is spread abroad, as simply as a
smile on a child's face.

52

Tired of waiting, you burst your bonds, impatient
flowers, before the winter had gone.
Glimpses of the unseen comer reached your wayside
watch, and you rushed out running and
panting, impulsive jasmines, troops of riotous roses.

You were the first to march to the breach of
death, your clamour of colour and perfume troubled
the air. You laughed and pressed and
pushed each other, bared your breast and dropped
in heaps.

The Summer will come in its time, sailing in
the floodtide of the south wind. But you never
counted slow moments to be sure of him.
You recklessly spent your all in the road, in the terrible
joy of faith.

You heard his footsteps from afar, and flung
your mantle of death for him to tread upon.
Your bonds break even before the rescuer is seen,
you make him your own ere he can come and
claim you.

53

CHAMPA
(From the Bengali of Satyendranath Datta)
I opened my bud when April breathed her last
and the summer scorched with kisses the unwilling
earth. I came half afraid and half curious,
like a mischievous imp peeping at a hermit's cell.

I heard the frightened whispers of the despoiled
woodland, and the *Kokil* gave voice to the languor
of the summer; through the fluttering leaf curtain of my
birth-chamber
I saw the world grim, grey, and haggard.

Yet boldly I came out strong with the faith
of youth, quaffed the fiery wine from the glowing
bowl of the sky, and proudly saluted the morning,
I, the champa flower, who carry the perfume
of the sun in my heart.

54

In the beginning of time, there rose from the churning of God's dream two women. One is the dancer at the court of paradise, the desired of men, she who laughs and plucks the minds of the wise from their cold meditations and of fools from their emptiness; and scatters them like seeds with careless hands in the extravagant winds of March, in the flowering frenzy of May.

The other is the crowned queen of heaven, the mother, throned on the fullness of golden autumn; she who in the harvest-time brings straying hearts to the smile sweet as tears, the beauty deep as the sea of silence,—brings them to the temple of the Unknown, at the holy confluence of Life and Death.

55

The noonday air is quivering, like gauzy wings
of a dragon-fly. Roofs of the village huts brood
birdlike over the drowsy households, while a
Kokil sings unseen from its leafy loneliness.

The fresh liquid notes drop upon the tuneless
toil of the human crowd, adding music to lovers'
whispers, to mothers' kisses, to children's laughter.
They flow over our thoughts, like a stream over
pebbles, rounding them in beauty every unconscious
moment.

56

The evening was lonely for me, and I was reading a book till my heart became dry, and it seemed to me that beauty was a thing fashioned by the traders in words. Tired I shut the book and snuffed the candle. In a moment the room was flooded with moonlight.

Spirit of Beauty, how could you, whose radiance overbrims the sky, stand hidden behind a candle's tiny flame? How could a few vain words from a book rise like a mist, and veil her whose voice has hushed the heart of earth into ineffable calm.'

57

This autumn is mine, for she was rocked in my heart. The glistening bells of her anklets rang in my blood, and her misty veil fluttered in my breath. I know the touch of her blown hair in all my dreams. She is abroad in the trembling leaves that danced in my life-throbs, and her eyes that smile from the blue sky drank their light from me.

58

Things throng and laugh loud in the sky; the
sands and dust dance and whirl like children.
Man's mind is aroused by their shouts; his
thoughts long to be the playmates of things.

Our dreams, drifting in the stream of the vague,
stretch their arms to clutch the earth, —
their efforts stiffen into bricks and stones, and thus
the city of man is built.

Voices come swarming from the past, — seeking
answers from the living moments.
Beats of their wings fill the air with tremulous shadows,
and sleepless thoughts in our minds leave their
nests to take flight across the desert of dimness,
in the passionate thirst for forms. They are
lampless pilgrims, seeking the shore of light,
to find themselves in things. They will be lured
into poet's rhymes, they will be housed in the
towers of the town not yet planned, they have
their call to arms from the battlefields of the
future, they are bidden to join hands in the strifes
of peace yet to come.

59

They do not build high towers in the Land of All-I-Have-Found. A grassy lawn runs by the road, with a stream of fugitive water at its side. The bees haunt the cottage porches abloom with passion flowers. The men set out on their errands with a smile, and in the evening they come home with a song, with no wages, in the Land of All-I-Have-Found.

In the midday, sitting in the cool of their courtyards, the women hum and spin at their wheels, while over the waving harvest comes wafted the music of shepherds' flutes. It rejoices the wayfarers^ hearts who walk singing through the shimmering shadows of the fragrant forest in the Land of All-I-Have-Found.

The traders sail with their merchandise down the river, but they do not moor their boats in this land; soldiers march with banners flying, but the king never stops his chariot. Travellers who come from afar to rest here awhile, go away without knowing what there is in the Land of All-I-Have-Found.

Here crowds do not jostle each other in the
roads. O poet, set up your house in this land.
Wash from your feet the dust of distant wanderings,
tune your lute, and at the day's end stretch
yourself on the cool grass under the evening star
in the Land of All-I-Have-Found.

60

Take back your coins, King's Councillor. I
am of those women you sent to the forest
shrine to decoy the young ascetic who had never seen
a woman. I failed in your bidding.

Dimly day was breaking when the hermit
boy came to bathe in the stream, his tawny locks
crowded on his shoulders, like a cluster of morning
clouds, and his limbs shining like a streak of
sunbeam. We laughed and sang as we rowed in
our boat; we jumped into the river in a mad
frolic, and danced around him, when the sun
rose staring at us from the water's edge in a flush
of divine anger.

Like a child-god, the boy opened his eyes and
watched our movements, the wonder deepening
till his eyes shone like morning stars. He lifted
his clasped hands and chanted a hymn of praise
in his bird-like young voice, thrilling every leaf
of the forest. Never such words were sung to a
mortal woman before; they were like the silent
hymn to the dawn which rises from the hushed
hills. The women hid their mouths with their

hands, their bodies swaying with laughter, and a spasm of doubt ran across his face. Quickly came I to his side, sorely pained, and, bowing to his feet, I said, "Lord, accept my service."

I led him to the grassy bank, wiped his body with the end of my silken mantle, and, kneeling on the ground, I dried his feet with my trailing hair. When I raised my face and looked into his eyes, I thought I felt the world's first kiss to the first woman,—Blessed am I, blessed is God, who made me a woman. I heard him say to me, "What God unknown are you.? Your touch is the touch of the Immortal, your eyes have the mystery of the midnight."

Ah, no, not that smile. King's Councillor, — the dust of worldly wisdom has covered your sight, old man. But this boy's innocence pierced the mist and saw the shining truth, the woman divine.

Ah, how the goddess wakened in me, at the awful light of that first adoration. Tears filled my eyes, the morning ray caressed my hair like a sister, and the woodland breeze kissed my forehead as it kisses the flowers.

The women clapped their hands, and laughed their obscene laugh, and with veils dragging on the dust and hair hanging loose, they began to pelt him with flowers.

Alas, my spotless sun, could not my shame
weave fiery mist to cover you in its folds? I fell
at his feet and cried, "Forgive me." I fled like
a stricken deer through shade and sun, and cried
as I fled, "Forgive me." The women's foul
laughter pressed me like a crackling fire, but
the words ever rang in my ears, "What God
unknown are you?"

CROSSING

1

The Sun breaks out from the clouds on the day
when I must go.

And the sky gazes upon the earth like God's wonder.

My heart is sad, for it knows not from where
comes its call.

Does the breeze bring the whisper of the world
which I leave behind with its music of tears
melting in the sunny silence? or the breath
of the island in the faraway sea basking in
the Summer of the unknown flowers?

2

When the market is over and they return homewards through the dusk,

I sit at the wayside to watch thee plying thy boat. Crossing the dark water with the sunset gleam upon thy sail;

I see thy silent figure standing at the helm and suddenly catch thy eyes gazing upon me;

I leave my song; and cry to thee to take me across.

3

The wind is up, I set my sail of songs.
Steersman, sit at the helm.
For my boat is fretting to be free, to dance in
the rhythm of the wind and water.

The day is spent, it is evening.
My friends of the shore have taken leave.
Loose the chain and heave the anchor, we sail by
the starlight.

The wind is stirred into the murmur of music
at this time of my departure.

Steersman, sit at the helm.

4

Accept me, my lord, accept me for this while.
Let those orphaned days that passed without
thee be forgotten.

Only spread this little moment wide across thy
lap, holding it under thy light.
I have wandered in pursuit of voices that drew
me yet led me nowhere.

Now let me sit in peace and listen to thy words
in the soul of my silence.

Do not turn away thy face from my heart's dark
secrets, but burn them till they are alight
with thy fire.

5

The scouts of a distant storm have pitched their
cloud-tents in the sky; the light has paled;
the air is damp with tears in the voiceless
shadows of the forest.

The peace of sadness is in my heart like the
brooding silence upon the master's lute
before the music begins.

My world is still with the expectation of the great
pain of thy coming into my life.

6

Thou hast done well, my lover, thou hast done well to send me thy fire of pain.

For my incense never yields its perfume till it burns, and my lamp is blind till it is lighted.

When my mind is numb its torpor must be stricken by thy love's lightning; and the very darkness that blots my world burns like a torch when set afire by thy thunder.

7

Deliver me from my own shadows, my lord,
from the wrecks and confusion of my days.

For the night is dark and thy pilgrim is blinded,
Hold thou my hand.
Deliver me from despair.
Touch with thy flame the lightless lamp of my
sorrow.
Waken my tired strength from its sleep.
Do not let me linger behind counting my losses.
Let the road sing to me of the house at every step.
For the night is dark, and thy pilgrim is blinded.
Hold thou my hand.

8

The lantern which I carry in my hand makes enemy of the darkness of the farther road.

And this wayside becomes a terror to me, where even the flowering tree frowns like a spectre of scowling menace; and the sound of my own steps comes back to me in the echo of muffled suspicion.

Therefore I pray for thy own morning light, when the far and the near will kiss each other and death and life will be one in love.

9

When thou savest me the steps are lighter in the march of thy worlds.

When stains are washed away from my heart it brightens the light of thy sun.

That the bud has not blossomed in beauty in my life spreads sadness in the heart of creation.

When the shroud of darkness will be lifted from my soul it will bring music to thy smile.

10

Thou hast given me thy love, filling the world
with thy gifts.

They are showered upon me when I do not know
them, for my heart is asleep and dark is the night.

Yet though lost in the cavern of my dreams I have
been thrilled with fitful gladness;

And I know that in return for the treasure of thy
great worlds thou wilt receive from me one
little flower of love in the morning when my
heart awakes.

11

My eyes have lost their sleep in watching; yet
if I do not meet thee still it is sweet to watch.

My heart sits in the shadow of the rains waiting
for thy love; if she is deprived still it is sweet
to hope.

They walk away in their different paths leaving
me behind; if I am alone still it is sweet to
listen for thy footsteps.

The wistful face of the earth weaving its autumn
mists wakens longing in my heart; if it is in
vain still it is sweet to feel the pain of longing.

12

Hold thy faith firm, my heart, the day will dawn.
The seed of promise is deep in the soil, it will sprout.

Sleep, like a bud, will open its heart to the light,
and the silence will find its voice.

The day is near when thy burden will become thy
gift, and thy sufferings will light up thy path.

13

The wedding hour is in the twilight, when the birds have sung their last and the winds are at rest on the waters, when the sunset spreads the carpet in the bridal chamber and the lamp is made ready to burn through the night.

Behind the silent dark walks the Unseen Comer and my heart trembles.

All songs are hushed, for the service will be read under the evening star.

14

In the night when noise is tired the murmur of
the sea fills the air.

The vagrant desires of the day come back to their
rest round the lighted lamp.

Love's play is stilled into worship, life's stream
touches the deep, and the world of
forms comes to its nest in the beauty beyond all forms.

15

Who is awake all alone in this sleeping earth, in the air drowsing among the moveless leaves? awake in the silent birds' nests, in the secret centres of the flower buds? awake in the throbbing stars of the night, in the depth of the pain of my being?

16

You came to my door in the dawn and sang; it angered me to be awakened from sleep, and you went away unheeded.

You came in the noon and asked for water; it vexed me in my work, and you were sent away with reproaches.

You came in the evening with your flaming torches.

You seemed to me like a terror and I shut my door.

Now in the midnight I sit alone in my lampless room and call you back whom I turned away in insult.

17

Pick up this life of mine from the dust.
Keep it under your eyes, in the palm of your
right hand.

Hold it up in the light, hide it under the shadow
of death; keep it in the casket of the night
with your stars, and then in the morning
let it find itself among flowers that blossom
in worship.

18

I know that this life, missing its ripeness in love,
is not altogether lost.

I know that the flowers that fade in the dawn,
the streams that strayed in the desert, are
not altogether lost.

I know that whatever lags behind in this life laden
with slowness is not altogether lost.

I know that my dreams that are still unfulfilled,
and my melodies still unstruck, are clinging
to some lute-strings of thine, and they are
not altogether lost.

19

You came to me in the wayward hours of spring
with flute songs and flowers.

You troubled my heart from ripples into waves,
rocking the red lotus of love.

You asked me to come out with you into the
secret of life.

But I fell asleep among the murmurous leaves of May.

When I woke the cloud gathered in the sky and
the dead leaves flitted in the wind.

Through the patter of rain I hear your nearing
footsteps and the cry to come out with you
into the secret of death.

I walk to your side and put my hand into yours,
while your eyes burn and water drips from
your hair.

20

The day is dim with rain.
Angry lightnings glance through the tattered
cloud-veils.

And the forest is like a caged lion shaking its
mane in despair.

On such a day amidst the winds beating their
wings, let me find my peace in thy presence.

For the sorrowing sky has shadowed my solitude,
to deepen the meaning of thy touch about
my heart.

21

On that night when the storm broke open my door
I did not know that you entered my room through
the ruins.
For the lamp was blown out, and it became dark;
I stretched my arms to the sky in search of help.
I lay on the dust waiting in the tumultuous dark
and I knew not that storm was your own banner.
When the morning came
I saw you standing upon the emptiness
that was spread over my house.

22

Is it the Destroyer who comes?
For the boisterous sea of tears heaves
in the floodtide of pain.
The crimson clouds run wild in the wind
lashed by lightning, and the thundering laughter
of the Mad is over the sky.
Life sits in the chariot crowned by Death.
Bring out your tribute to him of all that you have.
Do not hug your savings to your heart,
do not look behind.
Bend your head at his feet, trailing your hair in the dust.
Take to the road from this moment.
For the lamp is blown out and the house is desolate.
The storm winds scream through your doors,
the walls are rocking,
and the call comes from the land of dimness beyond your ken.
Hide not your face in terror; tears are in vain; your door chains have snapped.
Run out for your voyage
to the end of all joys and sorrows.
Let your steps be the steps of a desperate dance.
Sing "Victory to Life in Death."
Accept your destiny, O Bride !
Put on your red robe to follow through the darkness
the torchlight of the Bridegroom!

23

I CAME nearest to you, though I did not know it,—
when I came to hurt you.
I owned you at last as my master
when I fought against you to be defeated.
I merely made my debt to you burdensome
when I robbed you in secret.
I struggled in my pride against your current
only to feel all your force in my breast.
Rebelliously I put out the light in my house
and your sky surprised me with its stars.

24

Have you come
to me as my sorrow?
All the more I must cling to you.
Your face is veiled in the dark,
all the more I must see you.
At the blow of death from your hand
let my life leap up in a flame.
Tears flow from my eyes, —
let them flow round your feet in worship.
And let the pain in my breast speak to me
that you are still mine.

25

I HID myself to evade you.
Now that I am caught at last, strike me,
see if I flinch.
Finish the game for good.
If you win in the end, strip me of all
that I have.
I have had my laughter
and songs
in wayside booths
and stately halls, —
now that you have come into my life,
make me weep, see if you can break my heart.

26

When I awake in thy love
my night of ease will be ended.
Thy sunrise will touch my heart with its touchstone
of fire, and my voyage will begin
in its orbit of triumphant suffering.
I shall dare to take up death's challenge
and carry thy voice in the heart of mockery
and menace.
I shall bare my breast against the wrongs
hurled at thy children,
and take the risk of standing by thy side
where none but thee remains.

27

I AM the weary earth of summer bare of life and parched.
I wait for thy shower to come down in the night
when I open my breast and receive it in silence.
I long to give thee in return my songs and flowers.
But empty is my store, and only the deep sigh rises
from my heart through the withered grass.
But I know that thou wilt wait for the morning
when my hours will brim with their riches.

28

Come to me like summer cloud,
spreading thy showers from sky to sky.

Deepen the purple of the hills with thy majestic shadows,
quicken the languid forests into flowers,
and awaken in the hill-streams the fervour of the far-away quest.

Come to me like summer cloud,
stirring my heart with the promise of hidden life,
and the gladness of the green.

29

I HAVE met thee where the night
touches the edge of the day;
where the light startles the darkness into dawn,
and the waves carry the kiss of the one shore
to the other.

From the heart of the fathomless blue
comes one golden call, and across the dusk of tears
I try to gaze at thy face
and know not for certain
if thou art seen.

30

If love be denied me then why does the morning
break its heart in songs, and why are these whispers
that the south wind scatters among the new-born leaves?

If love be denied me then why does the midnight
bear in yearning silence the pain of the stars?

And why does this foolish heart recklessly launch its hope
on the sea whose end it does not know?

31

Only a portion of my gift is in this world,
the rest of it is in my dreams.

You, whoever elude my touch, come there in secret silence,
hiding your lamp.

I shall know you by the thrill in the darkness,
by the whisper of the unseen worlds,
by the breath of the unknown shore; —

I shall know you by the sudden delight of my heart
melting into sadness of tears.

32

I KNOW you will win my heart someday, my lover.

Through your stars you gaze deep into my dreams;

You send your secrets in your moonbeams to me,
and I muse and my eyes dim with tears.

Your wooing is in the sunny sky thrilling in the tremulous leaves,
in the idle hours overflowing with shepherds' piping,
in the raindimmed dusk when the heart aches with its loneliness.

33

Someone has secretly left in my hand a flower of love.

Someone has stolen my heart and scattered it abroad in the sky.

I know not if I have found him or I am seeking him everywhere,
if it is a pang of bliss or of pain.

34

The rains sweep the sky from end to end.

In the wild wet wind the jasmines revel
in their own perfume.

There is a secret joy in the bosom of the night,
it is the joy of the veiled sky in its hidden stars,
the joy of the midnight forest in its hoarded bird-songs.

Let me fill my heart with it and carry it in secret through
the day.

35

When I travelled in the day I felt secure,
and I did not heed the wonder of thy road,
for I was proud of my speed;
thy own light stood between me and thy presence.

Now it is night, and I feel thy road at every step in the dark
and the scent of flowers filling the silence—
like mother's whisper to the child when the light is out.

I hold tight thy hand and thy touch is with me in my loneliness.

36

Sailing through the night I came to life's feast,
and the morning's golden goblet was filled
with light for me.

I sang in joy, I knew not who was the giver.

And I forgot to ask his name.

In the midday the dust grew hot
under my feet and the sun overhead.

Overcome by thirst I reached the well.

Water was poured to me.
I drank it.

And while I loved the ruby cup that was sweet as a kiss,
I did not see him who held it and forgot to ask his name.

In the weary evening I seek my way home.

My guide comes with a lamp
and beckons me.

I ask his name,
But I only see his light through the silence and feel
his smile filling the darkness.

37

Do not leave me and go, for it is night.
The road through the wilderness is lonely and dark
and lost in tangles:
The tired earth lies still, like one blind
and without a staff.
I seem to have waited for this moment for ages
to light my lamp and cull my flowers.
I have reached the brink of the shoreless sea
to take my plunge and lose myself for ever.

38

I DID not know that I had thy touch
before it was dawn.

The news has slowly reached me through my sleep,
and I open my eyes with its surprise of tears.

The sky seems full of whispers for me
and my limbs are bathed with songs.

My heart bends in worship like a dewladen flower,
and I feel the flood of my life rushing to the endless.

39

No guest had come to my house for long,
my doors were locked, my windows barred;
I thought my night would be lonely.

When I opened my eyes I found the darkness
had vanished.

I rose up and ran and saw the bolts of my gates all broken,
and through the open door your wind and light
waved their banner.

When I was a prisoner in my own house,
and the doors were shut, my heart ever planned to escape
and to wander.

Now at my broken gate, I sit still
and wait for your coming.

You keep me bound by my freedom.

40

Put out the lamps, my heart,
the lamps of your lonely night.
The call comes to you to open your doors,
for the morning light is abroad.
Leave your lute in the corner, my heart,
the lute of your lonely life.
The call comes to you to come out in silence,
for the morning sings your own songs.

41

Thy gift of the earliest flower came to me this morning,
and came the faint tuning of thy light.
I am a bee that has wallowed in the heart
of thy golden dawn,
My wings are radiant with its pollen.
I have found my place in the feast of songs
in thy April, and I am freed of my fetters
like the morning of its mist in a mere play.

42

Free me as free are the birds of the wilds,
the wanderers of unseen paths.
Free me as free are the deluge of rain,
and as the storm that shakes its locks
and rushes on to its unknown end.
Free me as free is the forest fire,
as is the thunder that laughs aloud
and hurls defiance to darkness.

43

When you called me I was asleep
under the shadows of my walls
and I did not hear you.
Then you struck me with your own hands
and wakened me in tears.
I started up to see that the sun had risen,
that the floodtide had brought the call of the deep,
and my boat was ready rocking on the dancing water.

44

Rejoice!
For Night's fetters have broken,
the dreams have vanished.
Thy word has rent its veils,
the buds of morning are opened;
awake, O sleeper!
Light's greetings spread from the East to the West,
And at the ramparts of the ruined prison rise
the paeans of Victory!

45

In this moment I see you seated
upon the morning's golden carpet.
The sun shines in your crown,
the stars drop at your feet,
the crowds come and bow to you and go,
and the poet sits speechless
in the corner.

46

My guest has come to my door
in this autumn morning.
Sing, my heart,
sing thy welcome!
Make thy song the song of the sunlit blue,
of the dew-damp air, of the lavish gold
of harvest fields,
of the laughter of the loud water.
Or stand mute before him for awhile gazing
at his face;
Then leave thy house and go out
with him in silence.

47

I LIVED on the shady side of the road and watched
my neighbours' gardens across the way revelling
in the sunshine.
I felt I was poor, and from door to door went
with my hunger.
The more they gave me from their careless abundance
the more I became aware
of my beggar's bowl.
Till one morning I awoke from my sleep
at the sudden opening of my door,
and you came and asked for alms.
In despair I broke the lid of my chest open
and was startled into finding
my own wealth.

48

Thou hast taken him to thine arms and crowned
him with death, him who ever waited
outside like a beggar at life's feast.
Thou hast put thy right hand on his failures
and kissed him with peace that stills
life's turbulent thirst.
Thou hast made him one with all kings
and with the ancient world of wisdom.

49

In the world's dusty road
I lost my heart,
but you picked it up in your hand.
I gleaned sorrow while seeking for joy,
but the sorrow which you sent to me
has turned to joy in my life.
My desires were scattered in pieces,
you gathered them and strung them
in your love.
And while I wandered from door to door,
every step led me to your gate.

50

I WAS with the crowd when I was in the road;
Where the road ends I find myself alone with you.
I knew not when my day dimmed into dusk
and my companions left me.
I knew not when your doors opened and I stood
surprised at my own heart's music.
But are there still traces of tears in my eyes
though the bed is made, the lamp is lit,
and we are alone, you and I?

51

When they came and clamoured and surrounded me
they hid thee from my sight.
I thought I would bring to thee my gifts
last of all.
Now that the day has waned,
and they have taken their dues
and left me alone,
I see thee standing at the door.
But I find I have no gift remaining to give,
and I hold both my hands up to thee.

52

Much have you given to me,
Yet I ask for more. —

I come to you not merely for the draught of water,
but for the spring;

Not for guidance to the door alone,
but to the Master's hall;
not only for the gift of love,
but for the lover himself.

53

I HAVE come to thee to take thy touch
before I begin my day.
Let thy eyes rest upon my eyes for awhile.
Let me take to my work the assurance
of thy comradeship, my friend.
Fill my mind with thy music to last
through the desert of noise!
Let thy Love's sunshine kiss the peaks
of my thoughts and linger in my life's valley
where the harvest ripens.

54

Stand before my eyes, and let thy glance
touch my songs into a flame.
Stand among thy stars and let me find kindled
in their lights my own fire of worship.
The earth is waiting at the world's wayside;
Stand upon the green mantle
she has flung upon thy path;
and let me feel in her grass and meadow
flowers the spread of my own salutation.
Stand in my lonely evening where my heart
watches alone;
fill her cup of solitude, and let me feel
in me the infinity of thy love.

55

Let thy love play upon my voice
and rest on my silence.
Let it pass through my heart
into all my movements.
Let thy love like stars shine
in the darkness of my sleep
and dawn in my awakening.
Let it burn in the flame of my desires
And flow in all currents of my own love.
Let me carry thy love in my life
as a harp does its music,
and give it back to thee at last with my life.

56

You hide yourself in your own glory, my King.

The sand-grain and the dew-drop are
more proudly apparent than yourself.

The world unabashed calls
all things its own that are yours—
yet it is never brought to shame.

You make room for us while standing
aside in silence;
therefore love lights her own lamp
to seek you and comes
to your worship unbidden.

57

When from the house of feast I came back home,
the spell of the midnight quieted
the dance in my blood.

My heart became silent at once
like a deserted theatre with its lamps out.

My mind crossed the dark and stood
among the stars, and I saw
that we were playing unafraid
in the silent courtyard
of our King's palace.

58

I WAS musing last night on my spendthrift days,
when I thought you spoke to me —

"In youth's careless career you kept
all the doors open in your house.

The world went in and out as it pleased —
the world with its dust, doubts, and disorder —
and with its music.

With the wild crowd I came
to you again and again unknown and unbidden.

Had you kept shut your doors in wise seclusion
how could I have found my way into your house?"

59

None needs be thrust aside to make room for you.
When love prepares your seat she prepares it for all.

Where the earthly King appears,
guards keep out the crowd, but when you come,
my King, the whole world comes in your wake.

60

With his morning songs he knocks
at our door bringing his greetings of sunrise.

With him we take our cattle to the fields and play
our flute in the shade.

We lose him to find him again and again
in the market crowd.

In the busy hour of the day
we come upon him of a sudden,
sitting on the wayside grass.

We march when he beats his drum,

We dance when he sings.

We stake our joys and sorrows to play
his game to the end.

He stands at the helm of our boat.

With him we rock on the perilous waves.

For him we light our lamp and wait when our day is done.

61

Run to his side as his comrades
where he works with all workers.

Sit around him as his partners
where he plays his games.

Follow him where he marches,
keeping step to the rhythm of his drumbeats.

Rush into the thick of the fair—
the fair of life and death —

For there he is with the crowd
in the heart of its tumult.

Do not falter in your journey across the lonely hills
over the thorns.

For his call sounds at every step
and we know that it is love's voice.

62

When bells sounded in your temple in the morning,
men and women hastened down the woodland path
with their offerings of fresh flowers.

But I lay on the grass in the shade
and let them pass by.

I think it was well that I was idle,
for then my flowers were in bud.

At the end of the day they have bloomed,
and I go to my evening worship.

63

My King's road that lies still before my house
makes my heart wistful.

It stretches its beckoning hand towards me;
its silence calls me out of my home;
with dumb entreaties it kisses my feet at
every step.

It leads me on I know not to what abandonment,
to what sudden gain or surprises of distress.

I know not where its windings end —

But my King's road that lies still before my house
makes my heart wistful.

64

While I walk to my King's house at the end of the day
the travellers come to ask me —

"What hast thou for King's tribute?"

I do not know what to show them or how to answer,
for I have merely this song.

My preparation is large in my house, where the claim is much
and many are the claimants.

65

My songs are the same as are the spring flowers,
they come from you.

Yet I bring these to you as my own.

You smile and accept them, and you are glad
at my joy of pride.

If my song flowers are frail and they fade and drop
in the dust, I shall never grieve.

66

My King, thou hast called me to play my flute at the roadside,
that they who bear the burden of voiceless life may stop
in their errands for a moment and sit and wonder
before the balcony of thy palace gate;
that they may see anew the ever old and find afresh
what is ever about them, and say,
"The flowers are in bloom, and the birds sing."

67

When my first early songs woke in my heart
I thought they were the playmates of the morning flowers.

When they shook their wings and flew into the wilderness
it seemed to me that they had the spirit of the summer
which comes down with a sudden thunder roar
to spend its all in laughter.

I thought that they had the mad call of the storm
to rush and lose their way beyond the sunset land.

But now when in the evening light I see the blue line of the shore,

I know my songs are the boat that has brought me to the harbour across the wild sea.

For absence is not loss in your hand, and the fugitive moments
that blossom in beauty are kept ever fresh in your wreath.

But when I come to my King's house I have only
this single song to offer it for his wreath.

68

There are numerous strings in your lute,
let me add my own among them.

Then when you smite your chords
my heart will break its silence
and my life will be one with your song.

Amidst your numberless stars
let me place my own little lamp.

In the dance of your festival of lights
my heart will throb and my life will be one with your smile.

69

Let my song be simple as the waking in the morning,
as the dripping of dew from the leaves,

Simple as the colours in clouds
and showers of rain in the midnight.

But my lute strings are newly strung
and they dart their notes like spears sharp in their newness.

Thus they miss the spirit of the wind
and hurt the light of the sky;
and these strains of my songs fight hard to push back thy own music.

70

I HAVE seen thee play thy music in life's dancing hall;
in the sudden leaf-burst of spring thy laughter has come to greet me;
and lying among field flowers I have heard in the grass thy whisper.

The child has brought to my house the message of thy hope,
and the woman the music of thy love.

Now I am waiting on the seashore to feel thee in death,
to find life's refrain back again in the star songs of the night.

71

I REMEMBER my childhood when the sunrise, like my play-fellow, would burst in to my bedside with its daily surprise of morning; when the faith in the marvellous bloomed like fresh flowers in my heart every day, looking into the face of the world in simple gladness; when insects, birds and beasts, the common weeds, grass and the clouds had their fullest value of wonder; when the patter of rain at night brought dreams from the fairyland, and mother's voice in the evening gave meaning to the stars.

And then I think of death, and the rise of the curtain and the new morning and my life awakened in its fresh surprise of love.

72

When my heart did not kiss thee in love, O world,
thy light missed its full splendour and thy sky watched
through the long night with its lighted lamp.

My heart came with her songs to thy side,
whispers were exchanged,
and she put her wreath on thy neck.

I know she has given thee something
which will be treasured with thy stars.

73

Thou hast given me thy seat at thy window from the early hour.

I have spoken to thy silent servants of the road running on thy errands,
and have sung with thy choir of the sky.

I have seen the sea in calm bearing its immeasurable silence,
and in storm struggling to break open its own mystery of depth.

I have watched the earth in its prodigal feast of youth,
and in its slow hours of brooding shadows.

Those who went to sow seeds have heard my greetings,
and those who brought their harvest home or their empty baskets
have passed by my songs.

Thus at last my day has ended and now in the evening
I sing my last song to say that I have loved thy world.

74

It has fallen upon me, the service of thy singer.

In my songs I have voiced thy spring flowers,
and given rhythm to thy rustling leaves.

I have sung into the hush of thy night and peace of thy morning.

The thrill of the first summer rains has passed into my tunes,
and the waving of the autumn harvest.

Let not my song cease at last, my Master, when thou breakest my heart
to come into my house, but let it burst into thy welcome.

75

Guests of my life. You came in the early dawn, and you in the night.
Your name was uttered by the Spring flowers and yours by the showers of rain.

You brought the harp into my house and you brought the lamp.

After you had taken your leave I found God's footprints on my floor.

Now when I am at the end of my pilgrimage I leave in the evening
flowers of worship my salutations to you all.

76

I FELT I saw your face, and I launched my boat in the dark.

Now the morning breaks in smiles and the spring flowers are in bloom.

Yet should the light fail and the flowers fade I will sail onward.

When you made mute signal to me the world slumbered and the darkness was bare.

Now the bells ring loud and the boat is laden with gold.

Yet should the bells become silent and my boat be empty I will sail onward.

Some boats have gone away and some are not ready, but I will not tarry behind.

The sails have filled, the birds come from the other shore.

Yet, if the sails droop, if the message of the shore be lost, I will sail onward.

77

"Traveller, where do you go?"

"I go to bathe in the sea in the redd'ning dawn, along the tree-bordered path."

"Traveller, where is that sea?"

"There where this river ends its course, where the dawn opens into morning, where the day droops to the dusk."

"Traveller, how many are they who come with you?"

"I know not how to count them. They are travelling all night with their lamps lit, they are singing all day through land and water."

"Traveller, how far is the sea?"

"How far is it we all ask?

The rolling roar of its water swells to the sky when we hush our talk.

It ever seems near yet far."

"Traveller, the sun is waxing strong."

"Yes, our journey is long and grievous.

Sing who are weary in spirit, sing who are timid of heart."

"Traveller, what if the night overtakes you?"

"We shall lie down to sleep till the new morning dawns with its songs,
and the call of the sea floats in the air."

78

Comrade of the road,

Here are my traveller's greetings to thee.

O Lord of my broken heart, of leave taking and loss, of the grey silence of the dayfall,

My greetings of the ruined house to thee!

O Light of the new-born morning,
Sun of the everlasting day,

My greetings of the undying hope to thee!

My guide,

1 am a wayfarer of an endless road.

My greetings of a wanderer to thee.

A short biography of Rabindranath Tagore

Rabindranath Tagore (nicknamed "Rabi") was born on 7 May 1861 in the Jorasanko mansion in Calcutta, the son of Debendranath Tagore and Sarada Devi. Tagore was the youngest of 13 surviving children.

Tagore was raised mostly by servants; his mother had died in his early childhood and his father travelled widely. But the Tagore family was at the arrowhead of the Bengal renaissance, publishing literary magazines; hosting theatre and recitals of Bengali and Western classical music featured there regularly. The boy Rabi grew up in the middle of literary-minded family members – and with visiting friends – with poems and songs and literary discussions mostly each and every day within the Tagore mansion.

A true poet who desired to be educated by Nature, Tagore largely avoided classroom schooling. His open school was his mind and the great teachers were the wind, the stars, the breeze and leaves and flowers.

Shelaidaha: 1878–1901

Because Tagore's father Debendranath wanted his son to become a barrister, Tagore had a brief stint at a public school in Brighton, East Sussex, England in 1878, after which he studied law at University College London, but again left. In 1880 he returned to Bengal degree-less, resolving to reconcile European novelty with Brahmo traditions, taking the best from each.

Tagore regularly published poems, stories, and novels after his return which had a profound impact within Bengal but could not carve a niche on the national. In 1883 he married 10-year-old (a common practice then) Mrinalini Devi, born Bhabatarini, 1873–1902. They were blessed with five children, two of whom died in childhood.

In 1890 Tagore was given to manage his vast ancestral estates in Shelaidaha (presently a region of Bangladesh); his wife and children joined him in 1898. Tagore released his *Manasi* poems two years later (1890). Tagore's duty was to travel up and down the Padma River in the luxurious family barge where he collected rents and blessed villagers who in turn honoured him with banquets—occasionally of dried rice and sour milk. His meeting Gagan Harkara proved fruitful for he introduced him to Baul Lalon Shah whose folk songs greatly influenced Tagore. The years 1891–1895 was Tagore's most productive ones for he could write more than half the stories of the three-volume, 84-story *Galpaguchchha*. The serious stories examined the vast poverty of an idealised rural Bengal.

Santiniketan: 1901–1932

Tagore moved to Santiniketan to found an ashram, an experimental school in the midst of groves of trees, gardens, a library. Here his wife and two of his children died. He received monthly payments as part of his inheritance and income from the Maharaja of Tripura, sales of his family's jewellery, his seaside bungalow in Puri, and a derisory 2,000 rupees in book royalties. By this time, he gained Bengali and foreign readers alike and published *Naivedya* (1901) and *Kheya* (1906) and translated poems into free verse.

In 1912, Tagore translated his 1910 work *Gitanjali* into English. While on a trip to London, he shared these poems with admirers including William Butler Yeats and Ezra Pound. London's India Society published the work in a limited edition, and the American magazine *Poetry* published a selection from *Gitanjali*. In November 1913, Tagore learned he had won that year's Nobel Prize in Literature: the Swedish Academy appreciated the idealistic—and for Westerners—accessible nature of a small body of his translated material focused on the 1912 *Gitanjali: Song Offerings*.

He was awarded a knighthood by King George V in the 1915 Birthday Honours, but Tagore renounced it after the 1919 Jallianwala Bagh massacre.

Twilight Years

Poetry from these fading years is among Tagore's finest. Suffering intensely with prolonged agony, Tagore passed away on 7 August 1941, aged 80. A. K. Sen, brother of the first chief election commissioner, received dictation from Tagore on 30 July 1941, a day prior to a scheduled operation: his last poem...

I'm lost in the middle of my birthday. I want my friends, their touch, with the earth's last love. I will take life's final offering, I will take the human's last blessing. Today my sack is empty. I have given completely whatever I had to give. In return if I receive anything—some love, some forgiveness—then I will take it with me when I step on the boat that crosses to the festival of the wordless end.

Travels

Between 1878 and 1932, Tagore travelled in more than thirty countries on five continents. In 1912, he took a sheaf of his translated works to England, where they gained attention from missionary and Gandhi protégé Charles F. Andrews, Irish poet William Butler Yeats, Ezra Pound, Robert Bridges, Ernest

Rhys, Thomas Sturge Moore, and others. Yeats wrote the preface to the English translation of *Gitanjali*.

Works

Known mostly for his poetry, Tagore wrote novels, essays, short stories, travelogues, dramas, and thousands of songs. Of Tagore's prose, his short stories are perhaps most highly regarded; he is indeed credited with originating the Bengali-language version of the genre. His works are frequently noted for their rhythmic, optimistic, and lyrical nature. Such stories mostly borrow from the lives of common people.

Tagore's non-fiction grappled with history, linguistics, and spirituality. He wrote autobiographies. His travelogues, essays, and lectures were compiled into several volumes, including *Europe Jatrir Patro* (*Letters from Europe*) and *Manusher Dhormo* (*The Religion of Man*). In 2011, Harvard University Press collaborated with Visva-Bharati University to publish *The Essential Tagore*, the largest anthology of Tagore's works available in English; it was edited by Fakrul Alam and Radha Chakravarthy and marks the 150th anniversary of Tagore's birth.

Drama

Tagore began penning plays at the age of sixteen, with his brother Jyotirindranath. He wrote his first original dramatic piece when he was twenty — *Valmiki Pratibha.* Later, Tagore's dramas used more philosophical and allegorical themes. The play *Dak Ghar* (*The Post Office*; 1912), describes the child Amal defying his stuffy and puerile confines by ultimately "falling asleep", hinting his physical death. Another is Tagore's *Chandalika* (*Untouchable Girl*), which was modelled on an ancient Buddhist legend describing how Ananda, the Gautama Buddha's disciple, asks a tribal girl for water. In *Raktakarabi* ("Red" or "Blood Oleanders") is an allegorical struggle against a kleptocrat king who rules over the residents of Yaksha puri.

Short stories

Tagore's trek down the path of short stories began in 1877 (he was only sixteen) with "Bhikharini" ("The Beggar Woman"). This was followed by *Galpaguchchha* (a collection of eighty-four stories) usually demonstrating Tagore's reflections upon his surroundings, on modern and fashionable ideas. Tagore typically associated his earliest stories (such as those of the "*Sadhana*" period) with an exuberance of vitality and spontaneity. Other stories followed soon: "Kabuliwala" ("The Fruitseller from Kabul", 1892), "Kshudita Pashan" ("The Hungry Stones", 1895), and "Atithi" ("The Runaway", 1895).

Novels

Tagore wrote eight novels and four novellas, among them *Chaturanga, Shesher Kobita, Char Odhay*, and *Noukadubi. Ghare Baire* (*The Home and the World*)—through the lens of the idealistic *zamindar* protagonist Nikhil—excoriates rising Indian nationalism, terrorism, and religious zeal in the *Swadeshi* movement. The end of the novel showcases Hindu-Muslim violence.

Shesher Kobita—translated twice as *Last Poem* and *Farewell Song*—is his most lyrical novel, with poems and rhythmic passages written by a poet protagonist. Tagore's novels brought novel attention by Ray and others adapting *Chokher Bali* and *Ghare Baire* into films.

Poetry

Tagore was the first non-European to receive a Nobel Prize in Literature and second non-European to receive a Nobel Prize after Theodore Roosevelt.

Tagore's poetic style was influenced by the atavistic mysticism of Vyasa and other *rishi*-authors of the Upanishads, the Bhakti-Sufi mystic Kabir, and Ramprasad Sen.

Tagore's most innovative and mature poetry embodies his exposure to Bengali rural folk music, which included mystic Baul ballads such as those of the bard Lalon.

Later, with the development of new poetic ideas in Bengal – many originating from younger poets seeking to break with Tagore's style – Tagore absorbed new poetic concepts, which allowed him to further develop a unique and international identity.

Songs (Rabindra Sangeet)

Tagore composed around 2,230 songs (rabindrasangeet) which merges fluidly into his literature, most of which—poems or parts of novels, stories, or plays alike—were lyricized.

Amar Shonar Bangla written in 1971 became the national anthem of Bangladesh. It was written – ironically – to protest the 1905 Partition of Bengal along communal lines: cutting off the Muslim-majority East Bengal from Hindu-dominated West Bengal was to avert a regional bloodbath. *Jana_Gana_Mana* includes the first of five stanzas of the Brahmo hymn *Bharot Bhagyo_Bidhata* that Tagore composed. It was first sung in 1911 at a Calcutta session of the Indian National Congress and was adopted in 1950 by the Constituent Assembly of the Republic of India as its national anthem.

Sri Lanka's National Anthem was inspired by his work.

Art works

Tagore took up drawing and painting at the age of sixty. Successful exhibitions of his many works were held throughout Europe. His keen sense of artistic knowledge coud beeasily made out in the simple artistic and rhythmic leitmotifs embellishing the scribbles, cross-outs, and word layouts of his manuscripts.

Next appeared his paintings which began to elude him unlike writing and music, playwriting and acting which came to him naturally. Yet he made an honest endeavour to master the art.

Repudiation of knighthood

Tagore renounced his knighthood in response to the Jallianwala Bagh massacre in 1919. In the repudiation letter to the Viceroy, Lord Chelmsford, he wrote

Santiniketan and Visva-Bharati

Tagore despised rote classroom schooling: in "The Parrot's Training". On visiting Santa Barbara in 1917, Tagore conceived to "make Santiniketan the connecting thread between India and the world [and] a world centre for the study of humanity somewhere beyond the limits of nation and geography."

The school, named Visva-Bharati, had its foundation stone laid on 24 December 1918. Tagore employed a *brahmacharya* system: *gurus* gave pupils personal guidance—emotional, intellectual, and spiritual. Teaching was often done under trees. He staffed the school, he contributed his Nobel Prize monies, and his duties as steward-mentor at Santiniketan kept him busy: mornings he taught classes; afternoons and evenings he wrote the students' textbooks. He fundraised widely for the school in Europe and the United States between 1919 and 1921.

But Tagore has been satisfied to the fullest with the original work of his poetry rather than their translation. Thus, to all of us, Tagore remains Kaviguru.

Last Five Years

Tagore's last five years were marked by chronic pain and two long periods of illness when Tagore lost consciousness in late 1937. He remained in death bed for some time. A similar spell followed in late 1940 from which he never recovered but his poetic pen was prolific during this prolonged suffering. A period of prolonged agony ended with Tagore's death on 7 August 1941, aged 80. He was confined in a room upstairs of the Jorasanko mansion where he had grown up. A. K. Sen, brother of the first chief election commissioner, received dictation from Tagore on 30 July 1941, a day prior to a scheduled operation: his last poem says this:

I'm lost in the middle of my birthday. I want my friends, their touch, with the earth's last love. I will take life's final offering, I will take the human's last blessing. Today my sack is empty. I have given completely whatever I had to give. In return if I receive anything—some love, some forgiveness—then I will take it with me when I step on the boat that crosses to the festival of the wordless end.

Black Eagle Books

www.blackeaglebooks.org
info@blackeaglebooks.org

Black Eagle Books, an independent publisher, was founded as a nonprofit organization in April, 2019. It is our mission to connect and engage the Indian diaspora and the world at large with the best of works of world literature published on a collaborative platform, with special emphasis on foregrounding Contemporary Classics and New Writing.

www.ingramcontent.com/pod-product-compliance
Lightning Source LLC
Chambersburg PA
CBHW020533080526
44583CB00013B/848